GALLIANO

GALLIANO

FASHION'S ENFANT TERRIBLE

DAVID FOY

UNICORN PRESS

Unicorn Publishing Group LLP

66 Charlotte Street

London

W1T 4QE

www.unicornpress.org

Published by Unicorn Press Ltd 2015

Text Copyright © David Foy 2015

Image copyright Getty Images or Rex images – see Photo Credits (page 128) for full details

ISBN 978-1-910065-65-5

10 9 8 7 6 5 4 3 2 1

Book design by Clare Faulkner

Printed in Slovenia on behalf of Latitude Press Ltd

ACKNOWLEDGEMENTS

Many thanks to Danny Lewis for the editing and Clare Faulkner at Small Dots for the amazing design work and overall look of the book.

At Getty Images many thanks to Toby Hopkins and Pat Lyttle.

The collaboration with London College of Fashion has been a huge part of the production of this book so I'd like to thank Jason Clapperton, Shaun Cole, Frances Odell and Katarina Rimarcikova for making the collaboration happen.

I worked with the following MA Graduate students on creating this book and their insight was invaluable. The teaching process was definitely a two way street.

Many thanks to Tian Chen, Sabrina-Maike Volz, Nothemba Mkhondo, Pilar Peña-Román, Sahiba Saluja and Yu Shi.

At Unicorn Press, I'd like to thank Simon Perks for the introduction, Lucy Duckworth for the enthusiasm and Ian Strathcarron and Eleanor Macnair for the advice.

frontispiece
The Fall/Winter 2007-08 ready-to-wear collection sees a deconstructed take on old Hollywood glamour with this all-white geometric evening wear dress.

CONTENTS

Behind every collection and dress is a mind-blowing fairytale and an artist's imagination run riot.'

INTRODUCTION

John Charles Galliano, CBE, was born into a devout Catholic family in Gibraltar on 28 November 1960. His origins were humble to say the least. Galliano's father, John Joseph, was a plumber and his mother, Ana Guillen Rueda, despite being an excellent seamstress and flamenco dancer, worked as a dinner lady as well as attending to the never-ending duties of being a mother and housewife. John Joseph, sensing a better life and more work opportunities, took the family (Galliano and his two sisters) to England when Galliano was six. The family moved around various districts in South London before settling at 126 Underhill Road, which lies roughly at the intersection between East Dulwich, Brockley and Peckham. These areas of London have since been gentrified to the point that they're unaffordable for the average Londoner, but during the time Galliano was growing up there – in the buzz of the late sixties – they were considered the mean streets of South London. Galliano wasn't a troublemaker, though; he tried his best to fit in with his new surroundings.

As an adolescent, Galliano attended Wilson's Grammar in Sutton. His experiences there as a young gay (yet closeted at home) teenager were somewhat typical for the times. Bullying and physical intimidation – with the teachers turning a blind eye – all figured in the daily routine.

Galliano left Wilson's in the late 70s with just a couple of O Levels and went to study on the design and textile programme at City and East College in Whitechapel. He complemented this first move into fashion by getting a weekend job at the Howies concession in the now world famous branch of Topshop on London's Oxford Circus. (The concession was co-owned by fashion PR guru Lynne Franks, who was allegedly the inspiration for the character of Edina in *Absolutely Fabulous*.) Life became a whirlwind of college, work at Howies and – as he moved further from the shy, retiring child he had

Galliano in silhouette at the Christian Dior Spring/Summer 2005 ready-to-wear fashion show in Paris, October 2004.

Galliano in a curious shot around the time of his graduation from Central Saint Martin's in 1984. Here he and model Jon Evans are wearing pieces and accessories from 'Afghanistan Repudiates Western Ideals,' a fashion collection that Galliano presented in July of the same year.

been on his arrival in London – nights out dancing in what was a legendary era for the West End clubbing scene.

The next port of call was Central Saint Martin's School of Art. Galliano's tutors at City and East had urged him to apply for the renowned school that, over the years, has brought through an amazing array of fashion talent, including Paul Smith and Rifat Ozbek. The school was – and still is – renowned for the diversity of its programme, which includes graphic art, film and fine art as well as fashion illustration, and it was here that Galliano really came into his own and began to feel at ease amongst his contemporaries (which must have been incredibly liberating after the stifling nature of his school life).

At Saint Martin's Galliano quickly earned the respect of his professors and his fellow pupils for his incredibly detailed drawings and illustrations. Illustration seemed to be where his passion lay, and it captured his imagination more than anything else at the time – so much so that for a while he strongly considered a career in that field. However, several influences during his time at the college steered him away from illustration and towards fashion design.

His experiences in London's clubbing scene started to play a huge creative part in Galliano's life. For club-goers, it was a big deal to try to create the most inventive or outlandish outfit for a night out at iconic (but sadly long-gone) venues such as the Blitz in Covent Garden, Cha-Cha, which was based in a back room of gay club Heaven, or, perhaps the most notorious, Taboo, where London's clubbers got their first sightings of Boy George and Leigh Bowery. This was also a time of experimentation with drugs of all kinds; it was almost as if you couldn't be part of the scene without trying *all* it had to offer.

Galliano also took on a part-time job as a dresser at the National Theatre. He worked for Dame Judi Dench and other actresses such as Zoë Wanamaker. Galliano soaked up the atmosphere of the theatre and observed how actors moved and used space, which would later inform how he put clothes together. The theatre also had a sense of drama and flamboyance that he lapped up and which he would later channel in his fashion shows.

Galliano was a hive of activity by this point. Studying at the college, working at the National Theatre, undertaking an internship at Tommy Nutter on Savile Row to learn tailoring, and, of course, the obligatory nights out in the clubs.

Apart from all this he was also exploring the books and fashion archives at Saint Martin's and at places like the Victoria and Albert Museum. It was in the latter that he first discovered the history of a post-revolution French royalist movement called Les Incroyables, and their look would become the inspiration for his first collection. The revolutionaries were using their choice of clothes to signal their social and political leanings. The male members of the movement wore pantaloons, over-sized neckties and earrings, and grew their hair long, which shocked conventional society. The women, named Les Merveilleuses, also aimed to shock by adopting the gowns and tunics of classical Greece and Rome. They would make these garments from linen or other materials that were as transparent as possible. The whole look outraged and disgusted Parisian society.

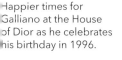

Happier times for Galliano at the House of Dior as he celebrates his birthday in 1996.

Galliano loved the passion and ideals of this ragamuffin group of revolutionaries, and it fired his creativity. He stayed up night after night trying out different ideas based on their style through his exceptionally detailed drawings. He even tried to channel the spirit of the times by drawing with an old fashioned calligraphy pen by candlelight on parchment paper soaked with tea.

Galliano now felt he had a strong enough theme around which to base his 1984 end-of-year show at Saint Martin's. He also knew that he would have to make the strongest possible impression in order to set him apart in what was an extremely competitive environment. Fortunately, to help him make his ideas reality, he was very adept at creating a team around him and fostering loyalty, so that people were willing to help him even if they were unpaid. For this show, his partner at the time, John Flett, helped with designing, cutting and sewing, while a team of friends and fellow students helped with sewing buttons and making the complicated jersey tubular skirts that were a feature of the collection. All were committed to helping him realise his vision, which was essential considering the lack of time and complete absence of a budget.

The School's show ran at the end of the summer term and that year it was to be held at the Jubilee Hall in Covent Garden. Galliano was chosen to be the closing act. Apart from the Saint Martin's crowd and Galliano's entourage from the club scene, there were also key industry types in the audience. One of these was Joan Burstein from Browns.

When Galliano's show finally started the audience were treated to a spectacle that would go down as one of the most memorable debuts in modern fashion history.

Breathtakingly beautiful multi-layered eighteenth-century blouses were accessorised with neckerchiefs and jodhpurs. Oversized coats were worn over the blouses for both menswear and womenswear and in fact it was hard to tell the difference between the sexes. The palette of colours made up mainly of white, black and grey was accentuated by the elaborate headdress and geisha style make-up of each model.

The pieces may have appeared to the untrained eye to have been simply referencing the historic, but to anyone who was part of the fashion scene at the time, the freshness with which Galliano had given the look a whole new breath of life caused intense excitement. It felt as though the audience were seeing a revolution in fashion unfold before their very eyes.

The sensation of the new didn't stop with the clothes. It extended to the models themselves, who flung themselves into the spirit of drama, interacting with the audience rather than simply being moving mannequins. Galliano had directed them to be as bold and proud as possible as he wanted every part of the show to stand out.

As soon as the show finished there was a scrum backstage to get Galliano's attention. Joan Burstein had been blown away by what she had seen and wanted to impress on Galliano how committed she was to his new vision. She did this in two ways: by buying the entire collection outright and by promising to show all the pieces in Browns' prime window site on South Molton Street in Mayfair. After arriving in store the next day – delivered by Galliano himself – the collection sold out in a matter of days.

Although this was an amazing feat it did create a problem. There simply wasn't any more stock to meet the demands of what was, through Browns, becoming a very clamorous, if at this point small, clientele. Galliano had to resort to relying on his ragtag band of helpers to try and fulfill orders. While the resultant clothes were at times amateur and haphazard, each was guaranteed to be unique … once they'd been finished at Galliano's parents' house.

'Burstein had been blown away by what she had seen and wanted to impress on Galliano how committed she was to his new vision.'

'Buyers from all over the world now sought to place orders – an amazing feat considering Galliano had only been out of college for six months.'

During this frenzied period a new collaborator emerged who would play a key role in Galliano's life. Amanda Harlech (née Grieve) was beautiful, intelligent and had a keen creative eye. She was just the sort of well-connected and well-bred society woman whose company Galliano craved. In this case the feeling was mutual. They met while Harlech was working as a junior fashion editor at *Harpers & Queen*. She had been looking for a collection that would stand out from the norm for a shoot she was working on and Galliano's old boss from his Saturday job at the Howie's concession, Lynne Franks, suggested Galliano to her. They hit it off immediately.

Aside from the *Harpers* shoot, Harlech was also working on the cover of a new Malcolm McLaren album, and it struck her that Galliano would be perfect to help her work on it. Perhaps inspired by meeting such an obvious creative soulmate, Galliano constructed a highly original piece – a fan made by tearing up pieces of old Japanese newspapers and then scribbling and drawing tiny symbols and text in gold and blood red ink all over it. Harlech loved it and knew she'd made the right choice in Galliano. A creative partnership was born that for a long time was one to be reckoned with in the world of fashion.

Things started to take a more structured and business-like turn when a fashion buyer from Copenhagen called Johann Brun came into the picture. He already had his own store but was checking out new styles and looks in London, where he saw Galliano's work. Brun was intrigued and approached Galliano about working together on a label. Galliano was at first reticent, given that he and his skeleton team were still struggling to fulfill all the Browns' orders, but Brun pursued the matter, securing agreement when he offered to finance Galliano, albeit on a modest scale at first. Amazingly, although probably typical for the time, there was no formal contract, just a handshake. The label would simply be called *John Galliano*.

With finance set up a more organised version of production got underway in the East End, where the team was now based. Galliano's first commercial collection was to be shown at London Fashion Week's Spring/Summer 1985 event, held at Olympia.

Galliano has always loved themes for his collection and the more obscure or wondrous the better. Prior to starting work on this second collection, he'd been reading about a period in Afghanistan during the 1920s when the Afghan King, after visiting London, had taken the radical step of encouraging his subjects to adopt the look of

Galliano with American *Vogue* Editor-in-chief Anna Wintour at the 'Le Monde De L'Art' party in Paris, 1993. Wintour has championed Galliano through good times and bad and has always taken a keen interest in his successive roles at Givenchy and Dior. Recently she has played a key part in Galliano's personal and creative re-emergence at Maison Margiela.

Western dress. This resulted in a fascinating blend of eastern tradition and western innovation in Afghan clothing.

Satisfied that he could curate a whole series of looks out of this one idea Galliano set about making the show as impressive as possible. He asked Amanda Harlech to style the show and she jumped at the chance. She even left her job at *Harpers & Queen* to commit herself full-time, such was her devotion to Galliano.

As usual, time was of the essence for the Galliano team. From dawn to dusk the East End studio was abuzz with the hand-dyeing of fabrics with highly unusual colours; the bleaching, smashing and taping together of accessories; cutting and sewing. The result was a collection of twenty pieces that showed a clever deconstructed sartorial subversion while playing on the idea of East meets West.

The effect of the show was to create the same sort of feeding frenzy that had erupted at the end of his degree show. Buyers from all over the world now sought to place orders – an amazing feat considering Galliano had only been out of college for six months. This enthusiasm among buyers meant that the first set of sales figures for the Galliano-Brun company showed a small profit, which at the time was no easy task in the world of fashion, particularly for such a new label.

Orders were now being sent out to prestigious retailers like Bergdorf Goodman in New York, so the team grew again with more assistants being taken on to help with knitwear and pattern cutting.

On a creative level Galliano felt he needed a muse. During one of his many nights out in the heady ambience of the West End club scene he came across a young woman from the Parisian upper classes called Sibylle de Saint Phalle. Like Harlech, she was Galliano's sort of woman, or at least the type he idealised. Aristocratic in attitude, well connected and with the right sort of education, she became the living doll upon whom Galliano could dress all his wildest ideas. Saint Phalle took to the role of muse as though the union had been pre-ordained.

Galliano wanted to do a much larger show for what was to become the Fall/Winter 1985–86 collection. The theme this time was 'the Ludic Game', which took its inspiration in part from Angela Carter's novel *Nights at the Circus*. The show was on 15 March 1985 and such was the demand for invitations the collection was shown twice. The music featured a jarring mix of scores from Italian horror movies and Irish rebel songs – the models were directed to imagine themselves in a fantastical storybook, and to run out onto the catwalk and dance a jig when the rebel songs came on. The overriding look was a haze of pre-Raphaelite luminosity overlapped with touches of Victoriana. As usual, the pieces were deconstructed, interchangeable and fluid. Outfits such as a double-breasted evening jacket with a Victorian bustle attached were inspired by nights out in the club scene, when Galliano would spot someone in a particular jacket, hat or skirt, then, taking that piece as a starting point, he would let his imagination run wild in the studio.

Reviews of the collection were somewhat mixed but that didn't stop the buyers from rushing to place orders, or from Team Galliano turning a profit again.

The next collection was called 'Fallen Angels' and aimed to mix the ethereal with pure romance. It was for Spring/Summer 1986, and was to be shown during October 1985 at London Fashion Week, which had by then moved to The Duke of York's Barracks off the Kings Road. Galliano's ideas had moved back to post-revolution France and he used this source of inspiration to create a look that was to be remembered as exceedingly romantic. It was also the first time he collaborated with shoe designer

Galliano and models at the John Galliano Boutique opening at Bergdorf Goodman, New York City, 1997.

Patrick Cox, although feathers were ruffled when Galliano instructed his models to do a circuit of the running track nearby to give the shoes a more distressed look.

Alongside his muse, Sibylle de Saint Phalle, who opened proceedings in a putty-coloured gown, the show featured models of many different nationalities, heights and ethnic backgrounds. It was a bold move for the time, when expectations were for identikit girls to walk the runway, but Galliano didn't care what the public perceived the classic model look to be. He either thought you were beautiful and should be there for all to see or you were just plain ugly – there was no grey area in the aesthetics of beauty as far as he was concerned.

The pieces featured sheer draping, soft palettes and empire waists for the women, while the menswear focused on precise yet deconstructed tailoring incorporating waistcoats and baggy coats.

The show's finale saw all the models being drenched with water so the fabrics clung sensuously to their bodies. Rapturous cheers from the crowd helped offset what was, once again, a less than enthusiastic response from the press.

The negativity didn't end there, though, as reports were making their way back to the workshop that buyers were experiencing fitting problems when receiving the final finished garments. This would remain an ongoing problem until Galliano was able to work with an established team at both Givenchy and Dior.

Things moved on rapidly in preparation for the Fall/Winter 1986–87 show to be presented in March 1986. This collection was called 'Forgotten Innocents' and would reflect upon the meaning of youth and a yearning for more innocent times. A press invitation was sent out featuring a young Helena Bonham-Carter who had recently starred in the movie *Lady Jane* about the tragic life of Lady Jane Grey, the de facto monarch of England executed in the sixteenth century. Galliano worked with his team to create a collection that included whimsical, delicate-looking crowns made from tarot cards and found objects from the street. There were also empire waists to set off

In April of 1998 Galliano accompanied Bernard Arnault, president of LVMH group, to this opening ceremony of its flagship Dior boutique in central Tokyo.

Galliano with esteemed fashion journalist Hilary Alexander at the party held for Colin McDowell's book on Galliano at Harrods in London, October 1997.

the dainty look of flowing dresses created from feathery fabrics, as well as oversized Victorian nightgowns and balloon-shaped coats embellished with fishtails. Imagine a gaggle of Romanov princesses let loose after finding a long lost dressing-up chest and you pretty much have the look.

Despite the hive of creativity and the non-stop cycle of design and production, things were coming unstuck behind the scenes and in the end Johan Brun called it a day in June 1986 – an announcement was made in the press announcing the dissolving of the partnership behind the *John Galliano* label. Galliano now had to start from scratch again, and search out a new financial backer.

He didn't wait around long and by July of that same year another announcement was made in the trade press heralding an agreement between Galliano and Peder Bertelsen of Aguecheck. The notice stated that Bertelsen would help fund one season only, namely Spring/Summer 1987. Galliano knew he was now being watched like a hawk and publicly stated that here was the new super-improved Galliano. He even smartened up his appearance to present something all together more sleek for the watching press and his contemporaries.

He had only eight weeks to get a collection together so got to work straight away. The studio for putting it together would be based in the stockroom of Aguecheek in Berkeley Square. As always there was an overriding theme for the collection. This time he sought inspiration from the film *Witness* that had come out a couple of years previously starring Harrison Ford and Kelly McGillis, who played a young Amish wife. Galliano loved the story of the film and saw in it a mirror of his own life, in terms of feeling like an outsider. To help create the look he wanted he hired a theatrical costumier from the English National Opera called Karen Crichton. Together they devised a dress silhouette that could work through the whole collection, with other pieces drawing their inspiration from that one core look. The show, when it was staged on 12 October 1986, was notable for being the first catwalk show that Naomi Campbell (still a Streatham schoolgirl at the time) did for Galliano. It was also his first unqualified success, with the press as well as the audience and the fashion buyers hailing his creations. The first models filed out to a Jeremy Healey soundtrack (who went on to provide the music for almost all of Galliano's subsequent shows), with their hair in Amish-esque styles to match the feel of the first set of outfits. These were followed by 1930s' style suits à la Marlene Dietrich (who always seemed to get a nod somewhere or other in these early shows).

Thanks to the success of the show Bertelsen drew up a contract that committed Galliano to a five-year partnership. He also wanted Galliano to have a more effective team to meet demand, and to that end new members joined the staff, while Karen Crichton also signed on permanently. The collaboration between Galliano and the costumier would prove a very creative and successful one. The whole team now moved to the top floor of a building in Shelton Street, which is situated on the border between Soho and Covent Garden, right in the heart of London.

The theme for the next collection also looked towards the movies but this time it was something more classic. Elia Kazan's film of Tennessee Williams's *A Streetcar Named Desire* was to be the key influence on the show. Galliano would certainly have found the drama of the piece appealing, but he may also, again, have seen parallels in the story with his own life. The plot follows Vivian Leigh's character, Blanche, turning up to stay with her sister, Stella, and Stella's brutish thug of a husband, Stanley. It seems a stretch to imagine that Galliano saw himself in Stanley, and it could have been a case of wish fulfillment, but the similarities between Amanda Harlech and the grounded and nurturing Stella, and similarity of Sibylle de Saint Phalle to the flighty yet detached Blanche obviously sparked Galliano's imagination.

The team started to produce a classically romantic collection that included gathered, pleated and whimsical day dresses in various pastel hues, along with fitted bodices, chiffon pieces and transparent wraparounds in organza. As ever with Galliano it was not a straightforward show with only one direction. An inspired suggestion had come from Harlech when she showed Galliano the long forgotten world of the Lady Edwardian Beekeeper, which he incorporated into the show and was a theme he came back to for later collections.

Again the style of Dietrich was represented, but the big difference this time came from Galliano's creation of three 'show' pieces. These were dresses that wouldn't go into the ready-to-wear collection but could only be commissioned to order as unique pieces fitted to the individual. They were to become known as the 'Shellfish' dresses (one of which is now in the permanent collection at the V&A) and they drew gasps of wonder as the audience took in the voluminous layered skirts made from pearl-grey organza that, when you saw them for the first time, took on the appearance of clamshells cascading

The haute couture
collection for Fall/
Winter 1999–2000
finds Galliano making
last-minute adjustments
before the models take
to the catwalk.

Galliano works on final adjustments to his Spring/Summer 2001 ready-to-wear collection in Paris, October 2000.

in a multitude of waves, one on top of another down to the ground. These breathtaking signature pieces had been worked on by Crichton and Galliano together, with Crichton building the structure of the skirt at home then bringing it to the studio for Galliano to add the finishing touches. The effect was a mesmerising mixture of 1950s' couture and a sublime fairytale take.

The show itself started with the soundtrack cranking up to a roar the song 'Stella' from Kazan's film, and then out came the outfits modelled with the now typical yet still novel theatrical flourish that had come to embody Galliano's shows. High waistlines were the order of the day, as were halter-top ball gowns that flattered and emphasised an exultant femininity.

The show was both a financial and critical hit. These were heady times for Galliano. Bertelsen's investment had so far gone well, a stronger team had been built around him to drive his work through and realise his creative ideas, the press and buyers were showering him with plaudits and, to top it all, Galliano was named British Designer of the Year for 1987.

After the unanimous success of the previous two collections and winning the award, Galliano decided he needed a new source of inspiration and possibly a change of scene. There had been a huge amount of stress producing so many high-octane shows, as well as the never-ending demand to come up with something new. For his next collection he looked to Paris, in particular pre-war Paris, taking inspiration from the Hungarian photographer Brassaï's photographs of the city during that era. Galliano saw Paris as full of romantic intrigue – a hotbed of debauchery, prostitution and a sense of style that oozed sensuality. The new collection was to be called 'Hairclips' (a reference to the bobbed and accessorised women's hairstyles of the time) with a look based on the bias-cut dress, which Crichton and Galliano had devised as the signature design that could work fluidly through the rest of the collection.

The stress of expectation and long hours of work at this time led to Galliano drinking more and more to cope. He was also experiencing problems with the mass production of the pieces he was creating, as well as trying to deal with the bickering and infighting between various factions within his team that had started to manifest itself and which was in danger of disabling the working process.

To try and distract himself from the increasing chaos around him, he decided to actually present the collection in Paris (in March 1990) not just to use the city for inspiration. At this point he was close to turning 30 and he felt an overwhelming desire to make his mark in what he felt to be the birthplace of couture. The show was to take place at the Cour Carrée at the Louvre. He worked non-stop to try and create a show and collection that would leave an indelible mark on the world of fashion.

The show included some references to previous Galliano collections, such as the reappearance of the Lady Edwardian Beekeeper look, while some of the models were

re-collection studio
hot of Galliano with
nodels in 2001.

At the end of the Fall/Winter 2002 haute couture Dior Collection, Galliano, with white feather headdress, emerges to give the audience the thumbs up.

doused in water, but in the main, the collection was startlingly novel. Red and silver satin was used in a series of classic princess coats with wide-cut collars, jodhpurs were teamed with waistcoats and delicate nipped-in jackets, while tight stirrup trousers and fencing outfits added to the sense of aristocratic sporting pursuit that ran through the show.

Galliano had been on edge throughout the run-up to the show and was nervous about the reaction, but the push towards Paris proved worthwhile, as the press response to the show was almost unanimously positive. However, there was little time to bask in the adulation. Galliano immediately put himself under pressure to outdo himself in subsequent collections.

He returned to the Cour Carrée for his Spring/Summer 1992 collection, which was presented in October 1991. It included eighteenth-century-style jackets, ruffles, brassieres with fine details in lace, satin-esque briefs and more bias-cut, this time in satin slip dresses. Quirky outsized picture hats and sombre clerical collars fought a battle at the opening of a show that contained flashes of nudity and generally had only a begrudging acknowledgement to modesty.

Despite the move to Paris and the momentum he was gaining in the fashion press for each collection there, Galliano's working life didn't stay calm; the recession in the UK caused Peder Bertelsen to stop providing the designer with financial backing.

Galliano wanted to stay in Paris (he had signed a lease on an apartment on Rue Vielle du Temple in the Marais district) and was concerned that not presenting another collection soon would see the momentum he had built up from the last two shows come to a halt. Determined to put on a show come what may, he secured an agreement to be allowed to use some studio space at the headquarters of Plein Sud, a French fashion label. Harlech and the rest of the team came over from London and work started on the new collection straight away.

With Harlech he conceived a vision of a fantastical pirate story and eventually gave the collection the name 'Filibusters'. It was to be presented on 14 October 1992 as part of the Spring/Summer 1993 show. In many ways it was a throwback to his 'Les Incroyables' collection from Saint Martin's but this time he was armed with a larger and altogether more professional team and it showed.

The audience gathered and sat in anticipation while the soundtrack of the film *JFK* blared through the sound system. Eventually (the show started two hours late!) the music switched to Jeremy Healey's set and the first series of deconstructed Napoleonic coats with fringed epaulettes appeared. Then came perfectly realised asymmetrical nightgown dresses in the smallest sizes possible, which contrasted with the extremely over-sized cuffs and splayed sleeves on several other pieces. The drama was heightened by the use of distressed American flags and swords, while bias-cut gowns were crowned with ravished satin corsets and exploding meringue-like sleeves. Then came the more streamlined elegance of the body-hugging cheongsam in classic blacks and reds. Given that the nudity in the previous show hadn't caused a backlash, Galliano used it again, with models' breasts popping out of glistening and sensuous gold strapless pieces (which may have distracted attention slightly from the intricate dragon motifs that had been embroidered on them).

In a way this show was Galliano's first experiment with the late nineteenth-century Chinoiserie movement and it clearly worked as reviews for the show were good and orders came flooding in.

However, despite this success Galliano didn't actually stage a new show till March 1993, due to financial uncertainty and failure to secure backing. His social circle was expanding, though, and he was soon an integral part of the social set in Paris. It was his deepening friendships with key players such as André Leon Talley, editor-at-large for *Vogue* magazine, which would help him put on his next show, with a disparate array of well-heeled supporters providing him with funding.

In the fall of 1993 Galliano again took on the task of trying to come up with something new and original as he got to work on a new collection for Spring/Summer 1994. Once more, the Louvre would provide the backdrop, and Galliano and Harlech set about finding inspiration to ensure the show was as spectacular as possible. Adept at combining influences from disparate sources, this time they managed to surpass themselves by creating a contrasting fantasy based on Russian and Scottish folklore. There had recently been news stories about DNA testing on the bones of the Romanovs, Imperial Russia's last ruling family, which had just been found on the outskirts of

Yekaterinburg in Russia. Galliano and Harlech had clearly got caught up in the romance of the lost daughters of the last Tsar of Russia and they created their own lost soul in the fictional character of Princess Lucrecia, who also had a few touches of Tolstoy's doomed Anna Karenina for good measure.

The show opened with the eerie howling of wolves; the first set of models then careered down the runway as though fleeing for their lives. The collection featured the definitive silhouette of Galliano's sumptuous yet tightly fitted eighteenth-century jackets and bias-cut skirts, which were fringed with handkerchief hems. It wasn't all sombre grandeur, though, as the more regimented and formal pieces were contrasted with playful mini kilts and cheeky ruffled bikini bottoms. To complete the sense of fatalism, models smoked while sauntering down the runway. It was Galliano at his gothic-storytelling best and the audience went wild for it.

Back in the day-to-day business of the fashion world, however, it was more a case of Dostoyevskian nightmare. Galliano still had no formal backer and the vacillations of unreliable cash flow meant orders were often not being delivered on time. Various concerned parties organised for Galliano to take a trip to New York in an attempt to rustle up a more stable financial arrangement. Whether by charm, luck or simply being in the right place at the right time, Galliano came back to Paris having secured an investment from a Swiss-born New York-based investment banker named John Bult and his partner Mark Rice. They had agreed to help fund his next show.

While (modest) backing may have been secured, all the backstage machinations to make it happen now left Galliano extremely short of time to actually prepare for his next show. In fact, he only had time to create eighteen new looks while budget restraints meant that the team had to use cheap black synthetic satin crêpe and use both sides of the material to try and create contrasting looks and layers.

The theme was the aesthetic of Japan seen through European eyes. Galliano started with a basis of 1940s' tailoring but mixed it up with the stylised drama and eccentric make-up of Japanese Kabuki theatre. He then further complicated matters by weaving in the ongoing story of Princess Lucrecia from his previous show. This time she had returned to her Paris home after the end of the First World War.

To incorporate all these wildly diverging themes the collection used 1920s' lingerie and kimonos with military touches, as well as furs and diamonds as accessories.

By this time the cult of the supermodel had been firmly established in the fashion world, and Galliano's show duly featured Kate Moss, Naomi Campbell, Christy Turlington, Linda Evangelista, Carla Bruni, Nadja Auermann and Helena Christiansen. This was no mean feat considering that there was almost no budget to pay them. However, the supermodels turned out in support of Galliano, as they all considered him a creative genius.

Socialite Sao Schlumberger lent her disused mansion as the venue for the show. Given the slightly awkward room sizes of the building and the oversubscribed guest list, Galliano actually staged the show twice. The onlookers were perched on randomly arranged gilded chairs and plush Victorian love seats. The Jeremy Healy soundtrack blared. First out and stalking the room was Carla Bruni. She sashayed past discarded chandeliers and leaves that had been artfully scattered by Harlech, demanding attention. The rest of show was a memorable tour de force seen through a haze of dry ice as first Campbell et al enthralled an audience made up of fashion editors, socialites and the demi-monde, then, after the Supers had made their exhilarating fly-by, other models refocused the audience's attention with trench coats, trouser suits and tuxedo jackets given an oriental twist.

Reviews were full of praise and sales orders were already being written up backstage in the Schlumberger mansion. This time the orders were coming from all the major retailers, including Bergdorf Goodman, Saks and Neiman Marcus in the US and Liberty's, Peter Jones and Harrods in the UK.

The response to the show prompted Bult and Rice to draft a more formal agreement and form a company with Galliano, giving him some much needed financial stability. A proper studio was set up, with both production and distribution moving to the Bastille area of Paris.

Galliano followed up his Japan-meets-Europe extravaganza with a much bigger show in October 1994 – bigger both in terms of budget (rumored to be $200,000) and size, featuring, as it did, 28 pieces. This was the memorable 'Pin Up' collection. Galliano also received his second Designer of the Year award from the British Council.

It was around this time that the possibility of Galliano going to Givenchy was first mooted. LVMH (Louis Vuitton Moët Hennessey) executives were cautious to say

Galliano and Sarah Jessica Parker at the Dior Spring/Summer show in 2004.

A Napoleon-esque
Galliano presents
himself on the runway
for the ready-to-wear
Fall/Winter 2005-06
collection in Paris,
January 2005.

Galliano was obsessed with creating shows and collections that grabbed the headlines every time – and that did so on a worldwide scale.'

the least, but were also intrigued at the thought of Galliano coming to Givenchy to revamp the label. Several clandestine meetings between Bernard Arnault (Chairman of LVMH) and Galliano were conducted before eventually and to much fanfare, Galliano's appointment as a Creative Director was announced – on the same day as Givenchy's last couture show of the season. Galliano was allowed to keep Harlech as part of his creative team, and he was fuelled with excitement at working at such a prestigious house. Little did he know how this particular association would end.

From 1995 the workload mounted up and up and Galliano would react by crashing and burning after the herculean task of creating not only a collection for Givenchy but also his own over and over again, year in year out. In his first season with Givenchy alone he had to design an haute couture collection for Spring/Summer 1996 as well as produce a 190-piece collection for the Fall/Winter 1996–97 ready-to-wear department, all in the space of two months. And on it went …

Shows got grander and more outlandish. Themes such as Native Americans and Ernest Hemingway's Spain would be presented to rapturous applause in such diverse locations as the Stade de France and the Equestrian centre in the Bois du Boulogne. For both himself and his new paymasters, Galliano was obsessed with creating shows and collections that grabbed the headlines every time – and that did so on a worldwide scale.

Things moved so quickly and successfully that in October 1996 LVMH announced that Galliano would be taking over the helm at the House of Dior, replacing Gianfranco Ferré. Alexander McQueen would replace Galliano at Givenchy. With these appointments, two of London fashion's bad boys would now be ruling the roost at two of Paris's oldest couture houses, a situation that wasn't exactly welcomed by everyone.

It was during this period that Harlech parted ways with Galliano.

Their friendship has been patched up since, but at the time the break was fractious, fuelled by what Harlech saw as Galliano's lack of fight to keep her when she received an offer from Karl Lagerfeld at Chanel. While Harlech had never actively pursued a working relationship with Lagerfeld, Galliano didn't seem to be making any moves to ensure she would be part of his new team at Dior.

The offer coincided with the end of Harlech's marriage and she needed to support herself and her two children. The offer from Chanel was financially attractive, but

Harlech wanted to stay at LVMH. However, when the executives failed to offer her a commensurate contract, she felt she had no choice but to leave, ending a ten-year working partnership with Galliano that had given them both so much exhilaration and creative fulfillment.

The theme of Galliano's first collection for Dior came from an intense period of trawling through the Dior archives. He went through every book, press clipping and old newspaper he could find, looking for the essence of what makes a Dior client and then working out how he could translate that into a new and memorable collection. Eventually he decided on bringing an old muse of Dior's, Germaine Bricard (generally just known as Mitzah), back to life. Here was the classic example of original chic just crying out for a rebirth on the modern runways of Paris. Mitzah was elegant, took lovers of her own choosing, had strong views on what was the right way of doing things, and had little time for those who might disagree.

Once Galliano had this central concept of the cult of Mitzah in place he embellished it with hints of Africa (in particular the Maasai tribes of Kenya), his understanding of Christian Dior himself, and the paintings of Giovanni Boldini.

So started the series of bold and beautiful collections that Galliano created for Dior, but also an even more demanding cycle of create, produce, show, enthrall – and then inevitable collapse from the exhaustion. True, in lots of ways Galliano didn't help himself with the constant partying, drugs and alcohol, but he was hardly the first person to go to such extremes. He would go through periods of using a personal trainer, and often turned up at shows all buffed up, a model of health and vitality, but it would be in sharp contrast to the extreme party lifestyle that worked as a temporary fix to the exhaustive drive to push himself to create something new and original time and again.

The collections themselves always gained maximum exposure in the press because of the storytelling and theatrics Galliano weaved into each show. Even though the trade press still occasionally sniped and felt that some of the pieces were just that, theatre, no one could argue with the sales figures and the continual growth of the House of Dior as a brand. Sales of handbags and perfumes (where the largest profit margins can be achieved) rocketed, while the number of Dior boutiques around the world grew and grew (and as far as LVMH – a business, after all – was concerned that was the true benchmark of success).

September 2007 and Galliano and former collaborator Amanda Harlech pose for the cameras at the *Golden Age of Couture* gala, at the Victoria and Albert Museum in London. The parting of ways when Harlech joined Karl Lagerfeld at Chanel had been a heart-wrenching decision for Harlech, but it's clear from this shot that the friendship survived.

Then on the evening of 24 February 2011 all it took was a matter of minutes to bring this story of creativity and success to come crashing down. The world now knows what came next and an inevitable and swift departure from Dior followed. There was no way Dior could have defended Galliano's choices on that day.

It would be very easy to end the story there, and for some people Galliano's actions on that day will be the thing that most sticks out in their mind. But for me that would be a mistake.

This book is not an analysis of Galliano's private life but a guide to how, why and when he created his visual masterpieces. Behind every collection and dress is a mind-blowing fairytale and an artist's imagination run riot. He is a fantastic example, when it comes to the art of the fashion designer, of a genuine rebel with a cause. From his first degree show to the sublime highlights achieved at Givenchy and Dior, he always pushed himself further and further, and was always hungry for knowledge – whether it was for inspiration or to reinvent an established style. With Galliano's work you might not always have liked what you saw, but you would never forget it.

JOHN GALLIANO
FALL/WINTER 1987

London, October 1987. An early, yet already highly polished, look at the John Galliano catwalk show. Galliano was now seen as the boy wonder of the London Fashion scene and this breakout collection was shown as part of London Fashion Week. The British Fashion Council also honoured Galliano for the first time that year, naming him British Designer Of The Year.

JOHN GALLIANO
FALL/WINTER 1989

A contrast of styles and finishes in Galliano's collection for London Fashion Week in October 1989. Nudity on the runway is a fairly common sight these days but this would have been considered fairly daring in the late eighties, especially as Galliano was now showing collections to a mainstream audience. What appears to be a simple sheer tunic is given an edge by the unusual choice of neckline that is neither a cowl, scoop nor keyhole but seems to draw the audience up to focus on the model's purposeful expression and curious wraparound mock-military hat with oversized flowers.

A young Helena Christensen on the runway from the same London Fashion Week show in October 1989. The fairly simplistic striped jacket and bunched up trousers is given an explosive African twist with the use of a glorious outsized gele headpiece and arm bracelets over the jacket.

JOHN GALLIANO
1990

Galliano had yearned to show a collection
in Paris, and to move on from his
London roots where he was starting to
feel frustrated. Biker girls and Galliano's
notion of the modern woman inspired
his debut in the French capital, staged
in a tent at the Louvre. The show was
a mix of satin princess coats with wide,
cut-out collars, as seen here mixed with
a beekeeping veiling, which was an idea
first given to Galliano by Amanda Harlech.
Other looks in the collection were
finished with cropped jackets, jodhpurs
and deconstructed sportswear, such
as fencing outfits and stirrup trousers.
A romance with Paris was born.

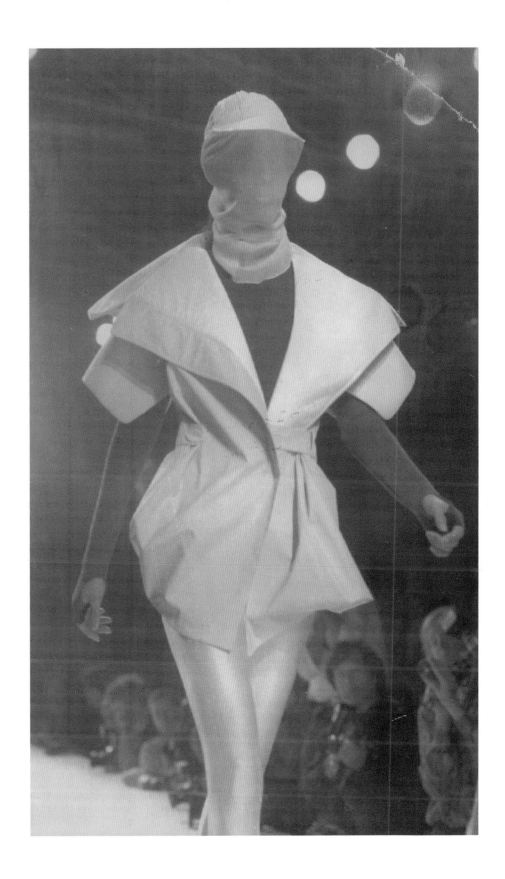

JOHN GALLIANO
SPRING/SUMMER 1992

Provocative and insolent. Ready-to-wear
Spring/Summer 1992.

JOHN GALLIANO
SPRING/SUMMER 1995
New York Fashion Week

Kate Moss wearing John Galliano.
Spring/Summer 1995 show at New York
Fashion Week held at Bergdorf Goodman
Department Store in New York.

Carla Bruni walking for Galliano in the same show at New York's Fashion Week held at the Bergdorf Goodman Department Store.

JOHN GALLIANO
for GIVENCHY
SPRING/SUMMER 1996

Paris 1996 and Galliano shows his haute couture Spring/Summer 1996 collection for Givenchy. The model struts the runway while holding a parasol with matching scarf.

In the same Spring/Summer 1996 Givenchy show this layered yet simple black skirt and matching black hat contrast effectively with the pearl bustier.

JOHN GALLIANO
for DIOR
FALL/WINTER 1997–98
ready-to-wear

An articulation of the Americana meets
Orient theme with this red mini bustier
dress and oversized fur bolero.

left From the same collection another master class in Orientalism with this ready-to-wear floor-length black and gold two piece.

right On the same note but without the oriental theme this playful yellow mini suit exudes a Chanel edge.

JOHN GALLIANO
for DIOR
FALL/WINTER 1997-98
haute couture

Naomi Campbell presents an Indian
dancing girl evening ensemble. A ruff
with bracelets and armlets in blackened
gold lamé compliments bra and sarong
miniskirt with choker.

JOHN GALLIANO
for DIOR
SPRING/SUMMER 1998

Linda Evangelista in an amethyst waffled crêpe bustier dress for the Spring/Summer 1998 ready-to-wear collections in Paris.

Carla Bruni in a black viscose-knit printed evening gown with spaghetti straps.

JOHN GALLIANO
for DIOR
FALL/WINTER 1998–99
ready-to-wear

A mixture of African tribal and London's
pearly queens for this patchwork
coat and matching hat as modelled
by Linda Evangelista during the
presentation of Galliano's ready-to-
wear Fall/Winter 1998–99 collection for
Christian Dior in Paris.

left Model Carolyn Murphy presents a leathery ensemble consisting of cutout leggings and skirt under a fur-trimmed open-front jacket in brown.

right The South America influence for this bright yellow, red and green coat is more than obvious. Note the ingenuous use of feathers with the outsized hoop frame.

JOHN GALLIANO
FALL/WINTER
1999–2000
ready-to-wear

Model Audrey Marnay presents a scarlet
fitted ensemble embellished with
flower brooches in primary colours and
matching handbag for the Fall/Winter
1999–2000 ready-to-wear collections
in Paris.

JOHN GALLIANO
for DIOR

A model presents a crimson dress
with kneepads while trailing
a billowing parachute-like train in the
surrounds of Versailles for the Christian
Dior Fall/Winter 1999–2000 haute
couture collection.

The audience at Versailles is wowed by this canary-yellow nylon strapped apron dress finished with a braided semi mohawk.

JOHN GALLIANO
for DIOR
SPRING/SUMMER 2000
ready-to-wear

A red star summer dress is matched with a splayed feathered hat featuring a semi veil. The ensemble is finished with a small messenger bag in the same material. Galliano for Christian Dior Spring/Summer 2000 ready-to-wear.

JOHN GALLIANO
for DIOR
SPRING/SUMMER 2000
haute couture

This ethereal and sublime creation taps
into the themes of ballet and mime as the
model poses in a diaphanous and sheer
piece. The only concession to colour here
is the pink neon-tubed headband. Part of
Galliano for Christian Dior haute couture
Spring/Summer 2000.

In a collection allegedly inspired by the homeless of Paris we see a model walk the runway in an olive organza, linen and gold lamé jacket with an olive lamé bias skirt.

left A ghostly procession along with the unusual mix of male and female models is an example from this controversial haute couture Spring/Summer 2000 collection. Galliano said he was influenced by the homeless of Paris and inspired by what he saw as their dignity in the way they embellished their daily lives.

right Burgundy again for this crocodile, silk taffeta and silk tulle coat paired with burgundy hand-painted corduroy pants.

JOHN GALLIANO
for DIOR
FALL/WINTER 2000-01

Actress Marisa Berenson graces the
Christian Dior haute couture Fall/
Winter catwalk with this deconstructed
Edwardian ensemble of white lace dress
with matching picture hat and veil.

JOHN GALLIANO
for DIOR
SPRING/SUMMER 2001

It's all about the money with this dollar insignia Warhol-esque t-shirt over a stretch net undershirt. Outfit is completed by a riot of colour and collage with the bolero jacket. Galliano for Christian Dior Spring/Summer 2001 ready-to-wear.

From the same collection we see the
contrast between a parachute bomber
bolero with panels using a highly
traditional pattern offset by a layered and
fringed skirt with just a hint of fishnet at
the bottom.

The model stands and poses in the spirit of anarchy and punk with a graffitied parasol. The outfit mixes printed leotard with minimal black sheer body mask and low slung skirt, which seemed to be the order of the day for this ready-to-wear collection.

JOHN GALLIANO
for DIOR
SPRING/SUMMER 2001

A model comes to an abrupt halt on
the runway to expose a provocative and
disarming ensemble of a maxi military
coat over a bunched domino print mini
slip dress teamed with knee-high Wonder
Woman boots for the John Galliano for
Christian Dior haute couture Spring/
Summer 2001 collection.

JOHN GALLIANO
for DIOR
FALL/WINTER 2001-02
ready-to-wear

A young and defiant Stella Tennant presents Galliano's quirky mix of checked prints, masculine tailoring, opulent furs and playful lingerie. All wrapped up with irreverent attitude.

Galliano's take on the rebel with a cause. High-waisted collage printed latex trousers are teamed with a bikini top whose knitted edges match the hat with elongated earmuffs.

JOHN GALLIANO
for DIOR
FALL/WINTER 2001-02
haute couture

The only nod to simplicity here is the flared denim hidden by the extraordinary Inca/patchwork hybrid coat that blends both folk and ethnic elements. Oversized puff sleeves contrast with fur finishes and leather cowboy chaps to reveal a remarkable colour composition in what is a perfectly styled ensemble.

The collection also saw the fusion of East and West in the form of this exquisitely embroidered silk oversized quilted wrap coat. The high-kitsch Asian motif pattern on the outerwear is teamed with a more classic red and white pattern on the inside lining. This blends oriental influences with the opulence of the European royal courts, giving an effect of volume and a unique shape.

JOHN GALLIANO
for DIOR
SPRING/SUMMER 2002

This collection still had hints of the Inca influence of the previous season, as shown in this multicoloured striped oversized clutch bag. The delicate tangerine hues in a rainbow effect on the silk dress are contrasted with the simple slip/stole poncho with lace edging. It's finished with a denim cowboy hat.

A grey herringbone tweed dress contrasts with a floating chiffon multicoloured blouse. The mix of contemporary prints and traditional fabrics brings the look together harmoniously.

JOHN GALLIANO
for DIOR
FALL/WINTER 2003-04

John Galliano for Christian Dior at
the haute couture Fall/Winter 2003–04
collection. Showgirl glamour here
with this sculptured bodice framed by
a long black wrap-coat creation with red
sequined glitter lining.

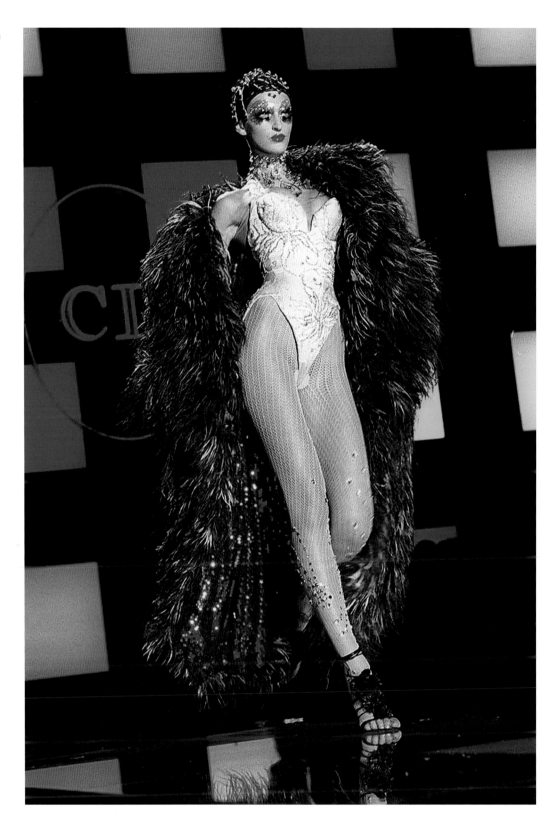

left Models come out at the end of
the Galliano for Christian Dior haute
couture collection.

right A game of opposites in this front-
loaded silver lamé geometric skirt. On
top, the model wears an emerald-green
embroidered velvet bolero jacket that
exudes the spirit of Spanish flamenco.

'It is important to remember where we come from,' stated Galliano when he was asked what the Dior Fall/Winter 2003–04 haute couture collection meant to him. Only one week after Galliano's father had passed away, his new show was a trip into his colourful childhood in Gibraltar and a tribute to the Galliano family's roots. The models strutted down the runway, wearing ruffled, parrot-green flamenco dresses, with tight, pleated corsets, as well as neckerchiefs and flat caps – all to the sound of castanets and tap-dancing.

JOHN GALLIANO
FALL/WINTER 2004-05

Paris fashion week in March 2004 and Russian model Anastasia Khozzisova presents what are two key themes of this collection – the notion of travel and a clash of cultures. Many of the ensembles for this show featured outsized hooped skirts embellished with traditional and indigenous motifs, as well as a folklore spirit throughout. Models carried or wheeled suitcases featuring the Galliano newsprint logo.

left This 18th century inspired gown, modelled by Nadejda Savcova, consists of a mantua teamed with a striking petticoat. The mantua, in combination with a crinoline skirt, enjoyed huge popularity during the late 17th and 18th century, and was often worn with a fontange. This look was also known as the robe á la française. The towering ivy headpiece, made by milliner Stephen Jones is accessorised with empty Coke cans. Along with the exceptional colour combination, it highlights the entire collection's bohemian influence.

right Another incredible outfit from the same collection. Amazingly this was actually the ready-to-wear show, not the haute couture collection. Note the use of cutlery in the amazing Stephen Jones headpiece.

Left Although intricate in its finish, this Galliano Gazette signature motif dress was actually one of the simpler outfits in this collection. Model Bea Elaine Fonseca wears tribal make-up and braided hair to contrast with the newspaper print. The use of the newspaper print first appeared in Galliano's Dior Spring/Summer 2000 haute couture collection, which is also known as the 'Haute Homeless' collection, and remains one of Galliano's most controversial shows.

Right A model wheels a shopping trolley plastered with the Galliano motif. Brazilian model Letícia Birkheuer wears an embroidered suede jacket with a fur collar as well as orange flower pants underneath a colourful knitted blanket and knitted pompon boots. Note the use of a tartan plastic holdall made into a bow attached to the trolley – a message to the world that something beautiful can be made from the mundane.

From the same collection, but with the
signature motif case now as headwear.

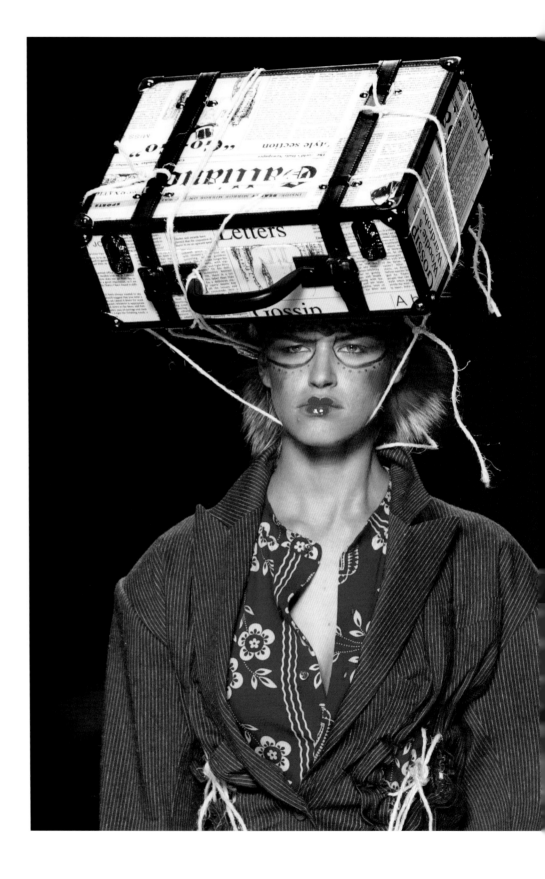

JOHN GALLIANO for DIOR
SPRING/SUMMER 2005

When Galliano was asked how he would describe the new Spring/Summer 2005 Dior haute couture collection he was quoted as saying that Bob Dylan's 'Like a Rolling Stone' was a major influence, as he loved the concept of 'Andy Warhol as Napoleon in rags!' What resulted was a mix of sixties-shaped mini dresses and Lady Josephine inspired gowns. Here model Alek Wek wears a combination of pointed knee boots with a rosé damask coat as well as a matching cavalier hat.

Left Galliano described his haute couture Fall/Winter 2005 collection for Dior as 'Andy Warhol is Napoleon in rags'. Taking inspiration from Napoleon's wife Josephine, the models glided along the runway in romantic, richly embroidered draped silk gowns framed in sumptuous silhouettes. The two outfits here almost mirror each other in their use of Russian Gzhel motifs on the edging and the intricate headdresses. This piece was a thoughtful reconstruction of the 18th century sack-back gown with an empire line, and the adorned chandelier-ridden birdcage hairstyles were inspired by the 18th century headdresses known as fontanges.

Right A Gainsborough muse reimagined by Galliano for this sumptuous piece of haute couture constructed with a multitude of fabrics and finishes.

JOHN GALLIANO
FALL/WINTER 2005-06

Sometimes it's a case of the simpler the better. This ready-to-wear mohair jersey dress with slashes could be a nod to the spirit of Brigitte Bardot but was actually inspired by Andy Warhol's muse, Edie Sedgwick. The monochrome striped dress is finished with extra long sleeves, and the whole ensemble is given an extra edge by the black crocodile mod cap.

JOHN GALLIANO
for DIOR
FALL/WINTER 2005-06

Diaphanous and ethereal couture confection, as modeled by Linda Evangelista, with this intricately beaded silk tulle dress for the Christian Dior haute couture Fall/Winter 2005–06 collection. Galliano paid homage to the history of the house of Dior, by dedicating this collection to Dior's romantic, sheer and flowing silhouettes.

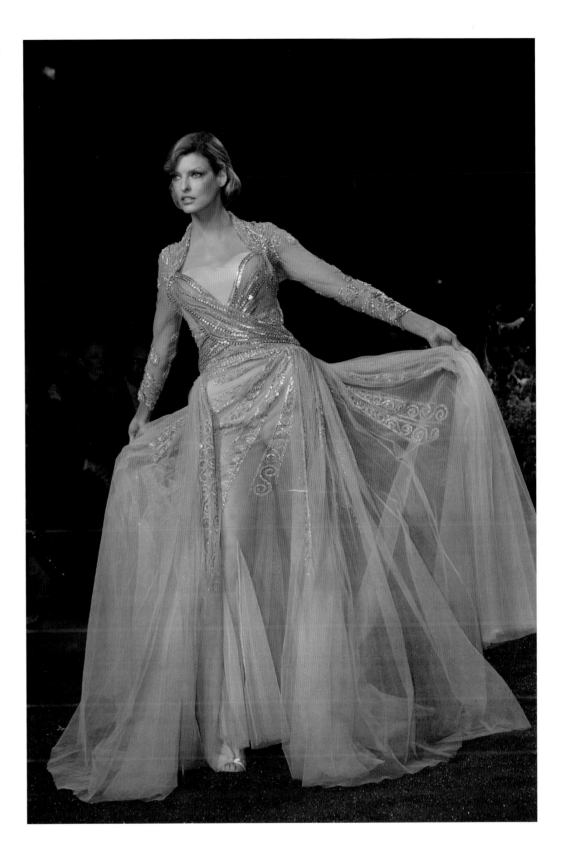

Underwear as outerwear in this delicate
lingerie dress structured over a cream
bodice with native motif on both the
central panel and the band underneath.

JOHN GALLIANO
for DIOR
FALL/WINTER 2006-07

Paris Fashion Week sees the true essence of haute couture in this green sculptured two-piece with jewelled embellishment that extends across the entire piece, starting with the shoulder-pad/collar combination and working its way down to the gathered skirt. It is also seen on the exquisite matching hat.

left A diverse mix of materials and fabrics in Galliano's haute couture nod to steampunk. There are also references to bondage in the use of straps over the top half and the PVC in the accompanying hat. But perhaps the most amazing element is the mixed materials in the skirt that enhance the contrast between red and black.

right Galliano is known for drawing inspiration from the most unlikely places and in crafting grand narratives that inform his collections. This is haute couture in its purest form with a fantasy from the ocean – from the detailed make-up that highlights the delicately applied coral pattern that covers the dress to the layered bolero and its encrusted sleeves. The outfit is finished off playfully with a lobster claw hat.

left Erin O' Connor is Joan of Arc incarnate in battle-ready couture. This draped and ruched valley green and sky blue voluminous gown is worn with an ostrich plume-topped metal cap. The effect is one of fluidity due to the use of colour and the feathers in the headpiece.

right Paris Fashion Week, and Galliano's Fall/Winter 2006–07 collection saw the Dior woman in warrior-like attire. Joan of Arc meets Dior in this gold satin evening dress paired with body-hugging black leggings and brass armory. The black visor make-up is applied to contrast with the angelic face of the model.

Model Tiiu Kuik strides the catwalk at
the Dior haute couture show in Paris in
an extraordinary Grecian dress. Galliano
plays beautifully with embellishments
and flattering drapes in a delicate shade
of rose. A plumed helmet and chalk-white
make-up complete this theatrical look.

JOHN GALLIANO
for DIOR
SPRING/SUMMER 2007

The spirit of Japan is seen in the use
of Hokusai's 'The Great Wave' painting
in the lower half of this piece, but with
a twist of Alice in Wonderland, as seen
in the props on the runway. The model
almost appears to be swallowed whole by
the curled and crêped oversized collar.

left Lily Cole walks the show for
Galliano's Dior Spring/Summer 2007
collection channelling the inspiration
of Madame Butterfly. This crisp cream
and gold fabric blends into classic
origami folds giving it incredible texture.
Galliano's impeccable skills and eye for
the smallest detail were evident in this
entire collection.

right Galliano never fails to deliver
drama on the runway and model Marta
Berzkalna stands out in this extraordinary
kimono gown with puffed sleeves. Here
the influence of Madame Butterfly and the
spirit of the geisha are obvious.

Left Galliano played beautifully with drapes and volume in a series of wonderfully sculpted gowns for his Spring/Summer 2007 collection for Christian Dior. The geisha themed show was more about spectacle than wearability, and the model certainly steals the show with this stunning pleated gown. Adorning the model with a large fan and wooden branches in her hair, Galliano stayed true to his theatrical persona.

Right A highly original and deconstructed take on the classic look of the geisha. The ensemble keeps its original form in the use of the black floor-length dress with its branch and leaf gold motif, but then takes on a modern twist with black leather elbow length gloves and daring geometric finishes around the shoulder and legs.

JOHN GALLIANO
for DIOR
FALL/WINTER 2007-08

left Naomi Campbell owns any runway she deigns to adorn. Here the imperial tone is set with a fluid evening gown with a roman edge and the use of a crown headpiece with matching arm clasps.

right Haute couture at its most luxurious with this one-shoulder gown accompanied by a pair of elbow-length black leather gloves and fixed Venetian mask. The ensemble creates a vision of charm and confidence; perfect for the show's setting of the Orangery at Versailles.

JOHN GALLIANO
for DIOR
SPRING/SUMMER 2008

left This layered leopard print slip dress is finished with a semi-transparent white lace shoulder girdle. Further enhancement is made in the use of make-up, with a dark, berry-coloured lipstick, as well as exaggerated smoky eyes, which add to the projection of allure and mystery.

right The model as harlequin, but given a twist by the use of a Renaissance collar ruff and gathered ruffle skirt.

The Gothic versus the Catholic. A sense of mystery and drama comes from this adaptation of the classic Spanish mantilla accentuated by the use of the same colour scheme in the lipstick, finely arched eyebrows and eyeshadow. The collar and rose highlight the finished look.

JOHN GALLIANO
for DIOR
SPRING/SUMMER 2009

This baroque look was created using multi–layered sweeps with a repeating flower pattern, and brings to mind the spirit of a royal court. The boat neck gives the entire piece a perfect line on the model. Instead of using bright red in the material, Galliano has used a carmine hue to symbolise nobility and luxury.

left Although inspired by 17th century Dutch elements, Galliano uses full-skirted fifties shapes and a tight-waisted design to evoke a feeling of high romance. The use of repeated bowknots in various sizes adds a whimsical finishing touch.

right More use of the oversized lace collar, which is deployed here to decorate the bateau neck and cuffs. Galliano uses the black and white colour scheme to draw the audience's attention to the structure of the garment. A Juno-esque feeling of elegance is created in the finished ensemble.

left This bright red one-piece dress is divided into two parts by the red waistband to show contrast between the oversized sleeves and tight-fitting sweep. This is reinforced by the use of different materials above and below the waist.

right The nipped waist creates the perfect line and a visual feast for the audience. The exaggerated gauze hat gives a perfect feminine touch as well as picking up the colour on the dress.

The Spring/Summer 2009 collection at the Musée Rodin in Paris and what at first appears to be a beautiful yet simplistic dress needs a closer look to appreciate the detail. There is one colour tone throughout, but the skirt part of the dress has been cleverly layered and has delightful gathered touches at the waist. Note the use of a white feather-like headpiece seamlessly interwoven with the model's hair.

JOHN GALLIANO
MENSWEAR
SPRING/SUMMER 2009

A clash of themes and cultures for this menswear ensemble with its ironic Roman headwear, Egyptian motif T-shirt and layered belts over what appears to be a swaddling effect using the Galliano Gazette print motif.

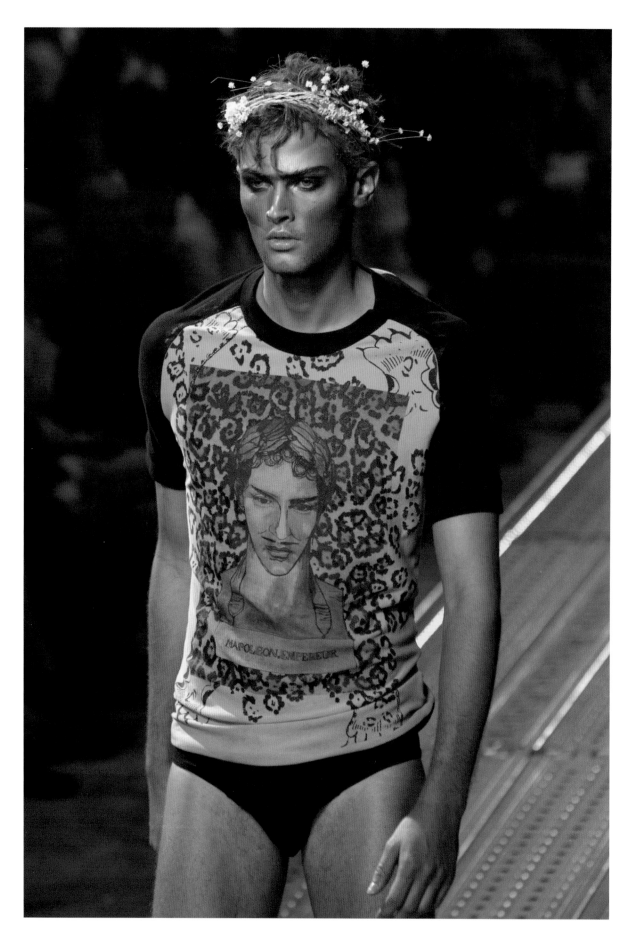

Left A model in underwear during the presentation of Galliano's Spring/Summer 2009 ready-to-wear menswear collection. Again he features amusing headwear, but the focus is on the irreverent T-shirt that exemplifies brand Galliano for the audience.

Right A mixture of the bold and the erotic in this three-piece of sheer club-wear tank top, black and gold underwear and roman sandals.

JOHN GALLIANO
for DIOR
FALL/WINTER 2011–12

left A model turns on the runway to show a perfect line elongated by the front-combed hairpiece. This simple but fun outfit uses a vivid red jacket to contrast perfectly with the white gathered petal skirt and grey leather gloves. The use of just three colours seems to heighten the vividness of the jacket even more.

right A haute couture masterpiece as seen at the Musée Rodin in Paris for the same collection. The black and smoky grey fringes twirl and cascade forming gathered rosettes at the bust and the top of the legs. The sombre nature of colour use in the outfit is highlighted by the riot of colour in the runway background and in the mirroring of aqua blue in the eye make-up and strappy sandals.

left Haute couture presented as a gift of nature with this playful tulip-themed gathered gown with stalk-coloured waist bow. The fuchsia visor highlights the sharpness of colour.

right A parade of striking primary colours as the models file out onto the runway at the end of the Christian Dior show as part of the Paris haute couture Fashion Week for Fall/Winter 2011–12 at the Musée Rodin in Paris.

Galliano poses for his rapt audience at the end of the same show.

With every Galliano collection, whether for his own label or other fashion houses, there is always a story.'

Galliano on his knees in the early 1990s pinning up a dress. The image was artfully posed to show Galliano amid the hubbub of the studio, but the truth is that he was much more likely to be directing the proceedings from afar, especially when production moved on to the loftier heights of the houses of Givenchy and Dior.

TEAM GALLIANO AND THE ART OF CREATIVITY

When one looks at a completed, fully realised collection by Galliano one has to consider the teamwork involved. His dreams and visions are brought to life by a diverse group of people that help and assist him in both the traditional and non-traditional sense. A milliner, a shoe designer and hair and make-up are all obvious members of this group, but the muse of the house (Amanda Harlech, for instance) can also spark the beginning of an idea that then leads to an entire collection.

Normally, once a collection has been shown Galliano will retreat from the public eye and regroup his energies and creative thoughts. Then he will return to start on the next collection, working solidly until it is complete and ready to show.

For Galliano this last stage in the process is much more than just showing a group of journalists, photographers and VIPs a collection of clothes – it's about creating a piece of theatre that acts as the perfect vehicle for those clothes to be seen by the world.

The Inspiration and the Story

With every Galliano collection, whether for his own label or other fashion houses, there is always a story. Sometimes the various and often wildly dramatic tales will connect with a diverse series of background themes and looks that Galliano revisits (think Asia, the Maasai of Africa or the drama of the French revolution for themes that have re-appeared over and over again). A character may come crashing down the runway, and seasoned fashion writers will know that this is a reference to a previous show (such as Princess Lucretia from his Spring/Summer 1994 collection).

Inspiration can come from the traditional route of research, as in his first collection for Dior when Galliano plundered the archives to try and find a muse so he could express his own vision through the classic silhouettes of Dior. Or he may see a news story that sparks his imagination, as in the case of Anna Andersen who claimed to be the long lost Russian Grand Duchess Anastasia. The next thing you know you see an entire collection played out against a thematic backdrop of the romance of Russia meeting the wilds of Scotland.

For the first ten years or so of his career Galliano would bounce these ideas off Amanda Harlech, or she would be the first to give him inspiration with a small item or a just a simple word. He would respond to her prompt and could end up creating an entire collection from something as small as a piece of material. An entire fairytale of couture would come from one word Harlech may have mentioned in passing to Galliano. Then a fully realised story would develop and that story would be passed along to the hat designer, the hair and make-up artists and to the models themselves just before they took that first step out onto the runway.

Staging the Scene

In the early part of his career Galliano was also indebted to Amanda Harlech for helping him dress the runways and rooms that showed his creations off to their very best. She not only planted the germs of ideas that would sprout into full-on extravaganzas, but she would be there, on her hands and knees or up a ladder, helping to create a stage to complement the spirit of each collection. From arranging the seats to make them more intimate, to sourcing and placing broken chandeliers and stringing up washing lines just so, Harlech made sure the art of pure theatre would form the perfect backdrop for Galliano's creations.

Even after Harlech made her move to work with Karl Lagerfeld at Chanel, Galliano continued to place a great deal of importance on providing the perfect stage to show his pieces in the best possible light. Set designer Jean-Luc Ardouin has worked with Galliano, notably when he designed a Cecil B. de Mille themed set for the Fall/Winter 1997 collection. He and others who followed soon learnt that a Galliano show would always require the maximum amount of commitment to achieve the biggest spectacle in the shortest amount of time. Authentic props would have to be sourced, lighting, health and safety issues worked out, and the assembly of the runway and set carefully planned so that everything the audience saw looked as though it had just casually come together and had always been there.

The Hats

The hats may not be for sale in Galliano's collections but without a doubt they form an integral part of every show. The milliner that everyone associates with Galliano is Stephen Jones. Jones started to work with Galliano from the time he made his first foray over to Paris and has provided hats for many of his shows for both Givenchy and Dior.

About a month before each show Galliano shares ideas and thoughts with Jones regarding the theme and ethos for this particular collection. There may not be an established set of illustrations at that point, but Galliano will usually know how many outfits he is going to show and in what order. From the conversations and briefings Jones will grasp what the spirit of the collection is going to be and gets to work. Then he sends sketches and ideas back to Paris – or wherever Galliano is working from – so that he can see those ideas and refine them. Once the final decisions have been made, the hats themselves can be produced, with the ultimate aim being that each hat is created to not only fully complement the collection but also to add a unique touch

above A typical scene in Galliano's office during the Dior Spring/Summer collection show in Paris, January 1997. Galliano is seen talking with Carla Bruni (long before her role as France's first lady). Monsieur Dior takes in proceedings from his photograph hanging between the two of them.

right Carla Bruni waiting while the final touches are given to this Maasai inspired creation just moments before the start of the Spring/Summer collection show in January 1997.

The final touches before a show. A model wears a picturesque creation by milliner Stephen Jones, inspired by 17th century Dutch still life paintings. This Fall/Winter 1999–2000 Dior haute couture collection, also known as the 'Matrix Collection' was a turning point for both modern fashion and Galliano himself, as he approached the new millennium.

to the look of each model hitting the runway. Jones himself will often be there on the
day of the show doing last-minute adjustments, securing his mini masterpieces on
the models and offering advice on how to wear the hat so as to project the essence of
the collection.

The Shoes

Just as important and sometimes even as theatrical are the shoes that are hand-made
for each collection. Galliano has collaborated with two well-known names in this field.
Galliano first noticed the work of Canadian-born shoe designer Patrick Cox at Vivienne
Westwood's Fall/Winter 1984–85 show. Galliano went on to collaborate with Cox on his
'Fallen Angels' collection that was shown at the Duke of York's Barracks on Kings Road.
Two different styles were created for that show, one a round-toed boot and the other
a deconstructed round-toed shoe. But, as ever, Galliano wanted a more unique touch
and that's when he instructed the models to cake the shoes in the mud from a nearby
running track.

Perhaps Galliano's best-known collaborator in terms of footwear is Manolo Blahnik.
Blahnik is renowned for his highly glamorous and ultra-feminine shoes and it's this
appreciation of what a woman wants that makes the match between him and Galliano
so perfect. The process that Blahnik goes through isn't as multifaceted as Jones' but it
still has the same aim in producing something that fully complements the model, the
dress and the entire collection.

Images and notes will go back and forth between him and Galliano, and from
those fragmented ideas Blahnik will get to work on producing examples for Galliano to
approve and add further embellishments to, before the final versions are produced.

The Invitation

No simple email or embossed card for Galliano. His invitations are themselves theatrical masterpieces. It's as though as much effort has gone into sending out these infamous bespoke invitations as into the collections themselves. More than anything else the invitation acts as a memento to sum up the spirit and essence of the collection that you are about to see.

Invitations have taken the form of 1920s' promotional boxing handbills, antique love letters, and a vintage Russian doll containing a charm bracelet, and have used such diverse detritus as (discharged) bullets, old keys and faded school reports.

Galliano is different in everything he does – from the way guests are seated to directing the models to give the audience as unique an experience as possible – so why should any less effort go into these couture keepsakes?

Hair and Make-up

Around the time that Galliano gets to work with Stephen Jones on the hats for a collection, he'll also be thinking about the hairstyles of the models. Sketches for each outfit will be finished and if the hat is near completion he'll want to make the hair or hairpiece complement the hat and work to create something fluid that, again, embodies the entire collection.

About three weeks before the show a hairdresser will come in and work in a similar way to Jones and Blahnik in that they will be told the story or theme of a show and shown sketches. The hairdresser will have their own thoughts and do their own research and then send those ideas back to Galliano for approval. Then a further three stages are undertaken. First a Galliano house model is asked to sit to represent the

Galliano is captured in his atelier. This is the starting point. From here his original inspiration is transformed into many works of art by the hands of skilled sewers and embroiderers, before making it onto the runway.

Galliano is seen here with leading British milliner, and good friend, Stephen Jones, at *The Golden Age of Couture* VIP Gala show at the V&A Museum in London. Over the years Galliano's and Jones's unique skills and sense of style have fused together to create many a catwalk spectacle.

collection while ideas are tried out. The second stage finds the hairdresser working on the individual look for each dress, and then in the last stage they will work on the individual models themselves. From this a series of hairpieces are created that embrace the vision of the collection and provide a finishing touch to each ensemble.

On the day of the show the work of the make-up artist is extremely important. A great make-up artist can elevate the final look of a show to one of perfection. The make-up artist will be there from the early hours, when the models first arrive. Over the previous four or five weeks they too will have been privy to the development of the overriding themes and storyboard of the show, so as to know which key palettes and hues to have ready. Galliano will want them to present as authentic as possible a look depending on the nature of the collection, such as the right use of colour for the historical era from which he is drawing inspiration.

GALLIANO AND THE WORLD OF CELEBRITY

As with any high profile designer, Galliano is no stranger to the world of celebrity.

One of the artists who has most often been associated with Galliano is Madonna. She has worn his pieces on various occasions, and not simply on the red carpet. When she filmed her video for 'Take a Bow', a single from her Bedtime Stories album, she was trying to project an image that might grab the attention of the producers of the upcoming film *Evita*. Galliano created a perfect nipped-in, classically Dior-esque look for her and Madonna indeed went on to win the role. Galliano followed up by creating various outfits for the film itself, as well as Madonna's ensemble for the premiere in LA and, later, for the 1997 Oscars ceremony, where she performed a song from the film's soundtrack.

Public attention was also focused on Galliano when Princess Diana was photographed in a blue bias-cut slip dress at the Met Gala in New York on 9 December 1996. This lingerie-inspired piece caused uproar at the time, with critics aghast that the Princess would be seen in what was considered a very risqué outfit, but her appearance in the dress went on to create a huge trend for similar looks. Both Diana and Galliano probably just considered all publicity to be good publicity.

The late 1990s proved to be a highly productive time for Galliano and in 1997 he created a dress that many saw as changing the course of red carpet fashion. The Chinoiserie chartreuse gown that Galliano had just shown as part of his first couture collection for Dior already had orders pending but Nicole Kidman contacted the house to see if they would be interested in dressing her for the Oscars, and she was happy to take direction from Galliano as to what would be the most suitable dress. Together they decided on the chartreuse piece with the perfect slim silhouette and touches of mink and chenille. At a time when most actresses on the red carpet were favoring pastels, it was a bold move on Kidman's part, but it set the precedent for red carpet events for years to come.

right One of Galliano's first forays back into the public domain was the creation of Kate Moss's vintage dress for her wedding to musician Jamie Hince in July 2011. In many ways Moss asking Galliano to create the dress was an obvious show of support from one fashion veteran to another, and from someone who understood the nature of scandal.

This classic gown was a mix of styles that gave a nod to both the 1920s and 1930s. Galliano's much favoured bias cut was deployed, but a simple, perfect silk slip dress and bodice served as the dress's focus. There were also delicate touches such as the sheer overlay embroidered with gold sequins and a train that was a masterpiece of couture sewing. Gold beading and rhinestones completed the feel of vintage glamour.

Galliano has twice created tour outfits for Kylie Minogue. In the early part of his career, in 1991, he worked on the wardrobe for her 'Let's Get To It' tour, while, more memorably, in 2005 he created a series of stunning, sexy pieces for her 'Showgirl' tour.

Kate Moss has long been associated with Galliano in the context of her runway and editorial work, but it was the moment that she chose to put their friendship in the spotlight that was most telling. Galliano had already fallen from grace in the earlier part of 2011 but Moss has never been one to be fazed by public opinion and rarely comments on such things anyway – actions speaks louder than words as far as she's concerned. Moss wanted a classic Galliano look for her wedding dress, but with as many couture touches as possible. At first they threw ideas back and forth on the phone until Galliano emerged from rehab for the first set of fittings. What resulted was a divine Jazz Age vintage classic.

The clothes – those wildly original, often jaw-dropping clothes – speak for themselves.'

CONCLUSION

May 2015, and Amal Clooney is dressed by Galliano for Maison Margiela at the Metropolitan Museum of Art in New York. Images of Mrs Clooney in this red strapless, floor-length dress were seen all over the world in seconds, prompting a keen debate about her choice of a Galliano dress. This piece sees a beautifully fitted peplum bodice in wet-look PVC tiered with lace to cascade down to a small train.

Galliano had made the decision to exhibit his first couture collection for Maison Martin Margiela on 12 January 2015 during London's Men's Collections. The show would be his long awaited return; as such it was the most anticipated of the whole event.

The crowd included fellow designers Christopher Bailey, Alber Elbaz, former partner Jasper Conran and Manolo Blahnik as well as photographers such as Paolo Roversi, Tim Walker, Nick Knight and Craig McDean. Friends, including Kate Moss and her husband, Jamie Hince, were there to give a show of support.

It was Galliano's first catwalk show since 2011. While it contained the drama and flair that the public had come to expect from Galliano, the timing was altogether subtler. It was scheduled for the end of the menswear run, sidestepping the normal rigidity of the Paris couture shows. This way he avoided any sort of conflict with his former employers at Dior. Galliano was hoping that the assembled editors, retailers and fashion observers would notice the sensitivity of the timing as well as the quality of the collection.

For some there was no great surprise in what Galliano presented but it wasn't a matter of playing safe. It was a reminder to anyone watching just what made Galliano a genius in the first place. There may not have been as many outfits as usual but what was there reminded journalists and buyers that here was a designer who still knew how to deconstruct, who was still a master of the art of tailoring, and who could deftly express luxury through the theatre of couture.

Galliano still knew how to leave a lasting impression. The show opened with a principal boy in harlequin leggings of black and flesh and ended with the vision of a ghostly empress, veiled and unable to speak due to the exquisite pearl and bronze mouth guard placed on her face. These two images bookending the show sent a strong message: Galliano still wanted to play but for now he knew he had to play by the rules.

The clothes themselves? It was a succinct collection that revolved around key pieces including a perfect black blazer, a mandarin-collared red velvet gown, and an immaculate tuxedo suit, but it wasn't a collection that was going to bring in the big orders, despite the nod to irony of the soundtrack including 'Big Spender'. It was actually a carefully thought out piece of theatre designed to enthrall, inspire and perhaps ask for forgiveness, no matter how brash and obvious some of the signals were.

Some observers commented that he should never have returned, that he'd had his time, had his chances and he blew it. That's a debate for another time and place. This book is intended as a reminder of what makes Galliano one of the most wildly imaginative and productive fashion designers of our time. Amongst these pages are examples of some of his best work where the riots of creativity and passion have been allowed to run free and magical stories have been told.

One of the most eye-catching pieces at the Margiela show was this red jacket, featuring an assortment of red lacquered shells gathered together haphazardly in the form of a breastplate. Inspired by the Renaissance and Giuseppe Arcimboldo, the circular translucent pockets and large cuffs add a touch of subtlety to this elaborate piece.

left Galliano has always been fascinated by the allure and art of the circus. In his debut collection for Margiela, he captures the playfulness at the heart of the house by bringing the ringmaster to the fashion circus with a deconstructed, off the shoulder double-breasted tuxedo jacket, draped over a scallop fringed skirt and black and white harlequin inspired leggings which are complemented by a feathered crown.

A new era for Galliano commenced with the announcement of his role at Maison Margiela. Groomed, sleek and immaculately tailored – in contrast to the heady days at Dior – Galliano seems to want the new collection to do the talking, rather than his own personality, which had so often been to the fore in the past. Here Galliano is seen with fellow designer Ronit Zilkha at the Connect fashion event held at the offices of accountancy firm BDO in London, May 2015. Galliano was there to meet rabbis from three of London's most influential synagogues. The synergy of reaching out to the Jewish community combined with his glorious return to Paris in July 2015 – for his first couture show in four years – reinforced Galliano's phoenix-like rise from the shameful ashes created in that same city in 2011. The show in Paris was still a humbled Galliano but there were flashes of cheeky brilliance and daring in the use of male models in what is traditionally a female domain. Here was an artist reborn and reinvigorated by the ability to express himself through the art of couture while still respecting the essence of his new house.

FURTHER READING

There are two really helpful and insightful books if you're looking to explore more about Galliano's history and background.

McDowell, Colin. *Galliano*. London: Weidenfeld and Nicolson, 1997.

Thomas, Dana. *Gods and Kings: The Rise and Fall of Alexander McQueen and John Galliano*. London: Penguin Random House UK, 2015.

PICTURE CREDITS